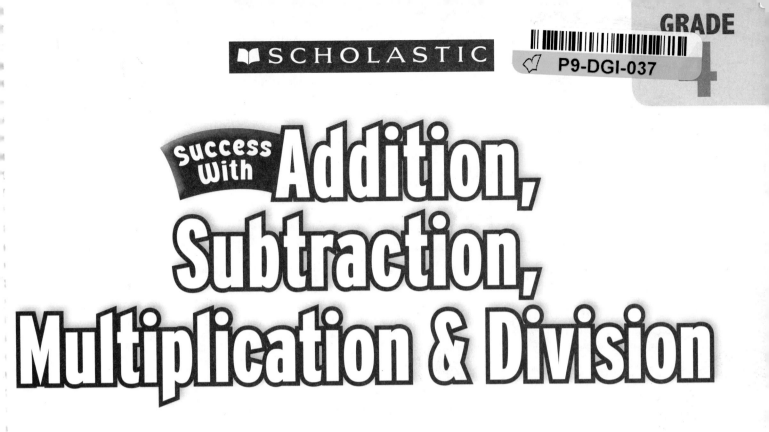

Success With Addition, Subtraction, Multiplication & Division

New York • Toronto • London • Auckland • Sydney
Mexico City • New Delhi • Hong Kong • Buenos Aires

Teaching *Resources*

State Standards Correlations

To find out how this book helps you meet your state's standards, log on to **www.scholastic.com/ssw**

Written by Lisa Molengraft
Cover design by Ka-Yeon Kim-Li
Interior illustrations by Sherri Neidigh
Interior design by Quack & Company

ISBN 978-0-545-20072-1

A-Mazing Eighteen

The answer to an addition problem is called the **sum**.

Find the path that leads from the mouse to the cheese by following the sums of eighteen. Add.

(5 + 4) + (3 + 6)	(7 + 6) + 5	(5 + 6) + (4 + 2)	(7 + 5) + 7	3 + (7 + 5)
4 + (6 + 6)	3 + (8 + 7)	(5 + 3) + (3 + 4)	(4 + 6) + 5	(5 + 9) + 3
(9 + 2) + 6	(5 + 3) + (6 + 4)	2 + (8 + 8)	8 + (6+ 2)	(4 + 5) + (2 + 5)
5 + (6 + 6)	(6 + 6) + (4 + 6)	(2 + 3) + (9 + 4)	3 + (7 + 5)	(6 + 7) + 6
(7 + 8) + 2	5 + (4 + 6)	7 + (4 + 7)	(5 + 6) + (4 + 3)	(8 + 4) + 6

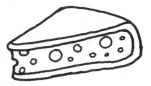

Write another number sentence with 18 as the sum. Do not use a number sentence from above.

Climbing High

To add multiple-digit numbers without regrouping, follow these steps.
1. Add the ones column.
2. Add the tens column.
3. Add the hundreds column.
4. Continue working through each column in order.

Add.

A.

$$1,136 + 2,433$$ $$9,025 + 851$$

B.

$$8,730 + 1,252$$ $$2,928 + 5,021$$ $$3,650 + 4,210$$ $$80,662 + 11,136$$

C.

$$55,100 + 31,892$$ $$60,439 + 30,310$$ $$81,763 + 8,231$$ $$36,034 + 41,753$$

D.

$$321,957 + 260,041$$ $$623,421 + 151,441$$ $$264,870 + 303,120$$ $$592,604 + 102,335$$ $$127,094 + 832,502$$

Mount Everest is the highest mountain in the world. To find the height of Mount Everest, begin climbing in Row D. Write the underlined numbers in order. Continue writing the numbers in Row C, Row B, and Row A. How many feet did you climb?

Reaching New Heights

To add multiple-digit numbers with regrouping, follow these steps.
1. Add the ones column.
2. If the sum is greater than 9, regroup to the tens column.
3. Add the tens column.
4. If the sum is greater than 9, regroup to the hundreds column.
5. Continue working through each column in order.

Which of these mountains is the tallest? To find out add. The sum with the greatest number in each row shows the height of the mountain in feet. Circle the height for each mountain.

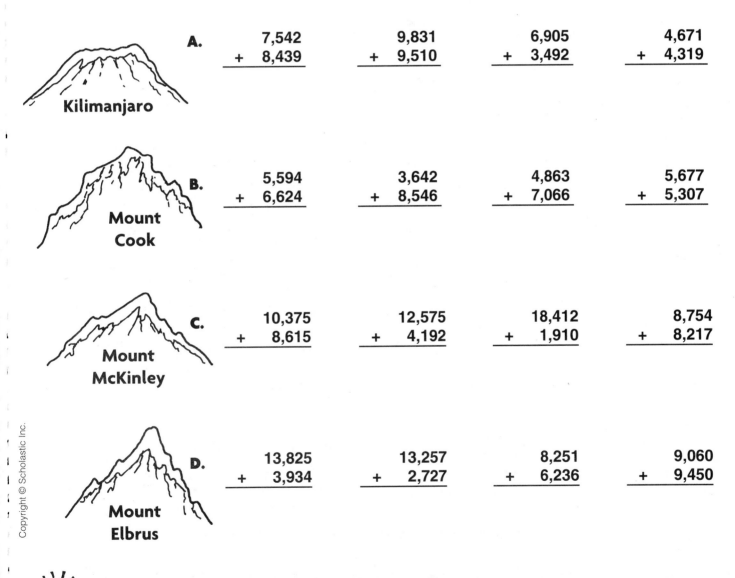

Kilimanjaro

A.

| 7,542 | 9,831 | 6,905 | 4,671 |
| + 8,439 | + 9,510 | + 3,492 | + 4,319 |

Mount Cook

B.

| 5,594 | 3,642 | 4,863 | 5,677 |
| + 6,624 | + 8,546 | + 7,066 | + 5,307 |

Mount McKinley

C.

| 10,375 | 12,575 | 18,412 | 8,754 |
| + 8,615 | + 4,192 | + 1,910 | + 8,217 |

Mount Elbrus

D.

| 13,825 | 13,257 | 8,251 | 9,060 |
| + 3,934 | + 2,727 | + 6,236 | + 9,450 |

Find the total height of the two mountains with the greatest heights.

Wild Bir(ds)

➡ *Some addition problems will require regrouping* [...] *al times. The steps look like this.*

1. Add the ones column. Regroup if needed.
2. Add the tens column. Regroup if needed.
3. Add the hundreds column. Regroup if needed.
4. Continue working through each column in order.

```
     1              11              111            111
   37,462         37,462          37,462         37,462
 +  22,798      +  22,798       +  22,798      +  22,798
 ─────────      ─────────       ─────────      ─────────
        0             60             260         60,260
```

Add. Then use the code to finish the fun fact below.

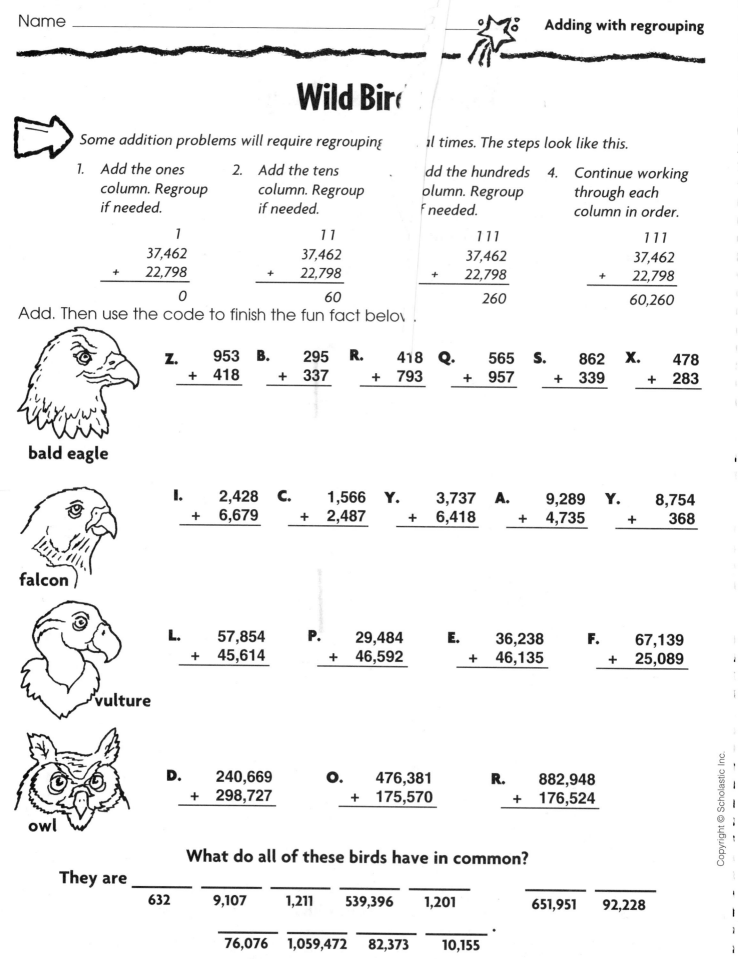

bald eagle

Z.	953 + 418	B.	295 + 337	R.	418 + 793	Q.	565 + 957	S.	862 + 339	X.	478 + 283

falcon

I.	2,428 + 6,679	C.	1,566 + 2,487	Y.	3,737 + 6,418	A.	9,289 + 4,735	Y.	8,754 + 368

vulture

L.	57,854 + 45,614	P.	29,484 + 46,592	E.	36,238 + 46,135	F.	67,139 + 25,089

owl

D.	240,669 + 298,727	O.	476,381 + 175,570	R.	882,948 + 176,524

What do all of these birds have in common?

They are ___ ___ ___ ___ ___   ___ ___
632   9,107   1,211   539,396   1,201   651,951   92,228

___ ___ ___ ___ .
76,076   1,059,472   82,373   10,155

The American Bald Eagle

To add numbers that require regrouping in more than one column, follow these steps.
1. Add the ones column. Regroup if needed.
2. Add the tens column. Regroup if needed.
4. Add the hundreds column. Regroup if needed.
5. Continue working through each column in order.

Add. Then use the code to finish the fun fact below.

H.	8,754 + 368	**L.**	7,789 + 4,759	**I.**	8,997 + 9,978
A.	8,599 + 8,932	**E.**	5,476 + 4,846	**O.**	9,475 + 7,725
C.	8,838 + 9,668	**T.**	6,867 + 7,256	**M.**	9,891 + 3,699

N.	92,854 + 37,898	**U.**	25,748 + 85,362	**Y.**	99,977 + 82,943	**R.**	57,544 + 78,587

The bald eagle is found ____ ____ ____ ____ ____ ____
17,200 130,752 12,548 182,920   17,200 130,752

____ ____ ____ ____ ____ ____ ____ ____
14,123 9,122 10,322   130,752 17,200 136,131 14,123 9,122

____ ____ ____ ____ ____ ____ ____ ____
17,531 13,590 10,322 136,131 18,975 18,506 17,531 130,752

____ ____ ____ ____ ____ ____ ____ ____ ____ .
18,506 17,200 130,752 14,123 18,975 130,752 10,322 130,752 14,123

Name _____

Funny Bone

➡ *Use the same steps to add several addends. Some columns will require regrouping, and some will not.*

Add. Then use the code to find the answer to the riddle below.

W.	T.	P.	N.	O.	E.
1,233 1,442 + 5,226	6,314 3,380 + 2,606	2,305 2,404 + 2,439	1,238 6,281 + 5,366	3,541 309 + 7,845	3,525 2,213 + 9,281

H.	R.	S.	!	A.	U.
444 7,283 + 8,217	4,327 4,331 + 1,746	4,024 678 + 4,505	5,441 421 + 3,954	2,653 3,338 + 2,924	5,560 4,202 + 1,541

What is the difference between a man and a running dog?

11,695   12,885   15,019

7,901   15,019   8,915   10,404   9,207

12,300   10,404   11,695   11,303   9,207   15,019   10,404   9,207

12,300   15,944   15,019

11,695   12,300   15,944   15,019   10,404

7,148   8,915   12,885   12,300   9,207   9,816

Canine Calculations

The numbers being added together are called **addends**.

Use the sum to help you find the missing numbers of each addend.

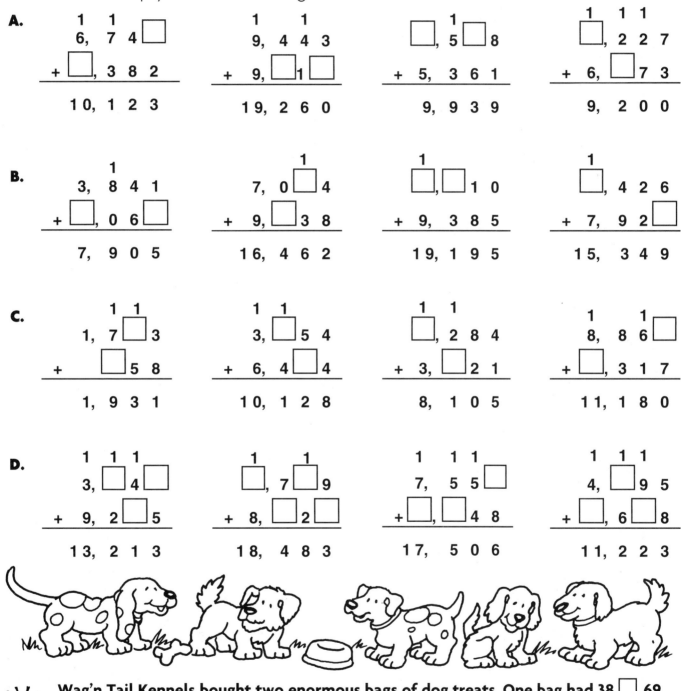

A.
```
    1 1
  6, 7 4 □
+ □, 3 8 2
-----------
 10, 1 2 3
```
```
    1     1
  9, 4 4 3
+ 9, □ 1 □
-----------
 19, 2 6 0
```
```
        1
 □, 5 □ 8
+ 5, 3 6 1
-----------
  9, 9 3 9
```
```
 1   1 1
 □, 2 2 7
+ 6, □ 7 3
-----------
  9, 2 0 0
```

B.
```
      1
  3, 8 4 1
+ □, 0 6 □
-----------
  7, 9 0 5
```
```
        1
  7, 0 □ 4
+ 9, □ 3 8
-----------
 16, 4 6 2
```
```
  1
 □, □ 1 0
+ 9, 3 8 5
-----------
 19, 1 9 5
```
```
  1
 □, 4 2 6
+ 7, 9 2 □
-----------
 15, 3 4 9
```

C.
```
    1 1
 1, 7 □ 3
+    □ 5 8
-----------
  1, 9 3 1
```
```
    1 1
 3, □ 5 4
+ 6, 4 □ 4
-----------
 10, 1 2 8
```
```
    1 1
 □, 2 8 4
+ 3, □ 2 1
-----------
  8, 1 0 5
```
```
        1   1
 8, 8 6 □
+ □, 3 1 7
-----------
 11, 1 8 0
```

D.
```
  1 1 1
 3, □ 4 □
+ 9, 2 □ 5
-----------
 13, 2 1 3
```
```
    1     1
 □, 7 □ 9
+ 8, □ 2 □
-----------
 18, 4 8 3
```
```
  1   1 1
 7, 5 5 □
+ □, □ 4 8
-----------
 17, 5 0 6
```
```
  1 1 1
 4, □ 9 5
+ □, 6 □ 8
-----------
 11, 2 2 3
```

Wag'n Tail Kennels bought two enormous bags of dog treats. One bag had 38,□69 dog treats in it. The other bag had 4□,510 pieces of dog treats. Altogether the bags had 80,879 treats. On another piece of paper, find the number of dog treats in each bag.

Money Fun

➡ *Remember to include a decimal point and a dollar sign in the answer when adding money.*

Add. Then use the code to answer the riddle below.

A.	$63.54 + 29.29	G.	$65.35 + 27.18	U.	$24.12 + 90.48	O.	$15.79 + 48.08

B.	$27.60 + 44.65	N.	$77.88 + 92.90	E.	$86.91 + 70.44	R.	$39.75 + 29.62

M.	$103.90 + 64.82	C.	$291.26 + 473.83	S.	$485.13 + 494.92	T.	$630.57 + 39.52

D.	$184.64 + 292.43	Y.	$354.60 + 261.74	F.	$964.36 + 252.04	W.	$904.86 + 95.82

Why are birds poor?

___ ___ ___ ___ ___ ___ ___
$72.25 $157.35 $765.09 $92.83 $114.60 $980.05 $157.35

___ ___ ___ ___ ___
$168.72 $63.87 $170.78 , $157.35 $616.34

___ ___ ___ ___ ___ ___ ___ ___ ___ ___
$477.07 $63.87 $157.35 $980.05 $170.78 $670.09 $92.53 $69.37 $63.87 $1,000.68
!

___ ___ ___ ___ ___ ___ ___
$63.87 $170.78 $670.09 $69.37 $157.35 $157.35 $980.05

A Penny Saved Is a Penny Earned

Write a number sentence for each problem. Solve.

A. Aimee and her 2 sisters are saving to buy a camera. Aimee has $12.89. Each of her sisters has $28.53. How much money do all the girls have combined?

B. Katie has $23.95 in her purse, $17.23 in her bank, and $76.82 in her savings account. What is the total amount of Katie's money?

C. Jonah worked in the yard for 3 days. The first day he earned $7.96. The second day he earned $2.00 more than the first day. The third day he earned $2.00 less than the first day. How much did Jonah earn altogether?

D. Jack has $9.29. He also has 79 dimes and 139 pennies. How much money does he have altogether?

E. Kelsey has 478 coins in her collection. The silver dollars equal $79.00, and the quarters equal $99.75. How much is Kelsey's collection worth in all?

F. Claire bought lemonade for herself and two friends. Each cup costs $1.75. How much did Claire spend in all?

On another piece of paper, write a word problem with a sum equal to $41.68.

Reach for the Stars

Always complete the operation inside the parentheses ( ) first.
Then complete the rest of the problem.

$(18 - 9) - 3 =$ _____ $18 - (9 - 3) =$ _____
$9 - 3 = 6$ $18 - 6 = 12$

Subtract. Then use the code to answer the question below.

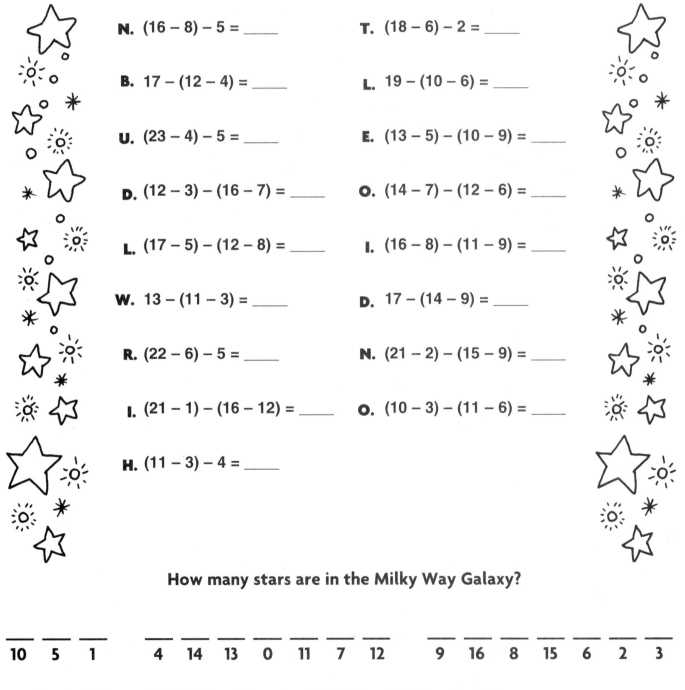

N. $(16 - 8) - 5 =$ _____   **T.** $(18 - 6) - 2 =$ _____

B. $17 - (12 - 4) =$ _____   **L.** $19 - (10 - 6) =$ _____

U. $(23 - 4) - 5 =$ _____   **E.** $(13 - 5) - (10 - 9) =$ _____

D. $(12 - 3) - (16 - 7) =$ _____   **O.** $(14 - 7) - (12 - 6) =$ _____

L. $(17 - 5) - (12 - 8) =$ _____   **I.** $(16 - 8) - (11 - 9) =$ _____

W. $13 - (11 - 3) =$ _____   **D.** $17 - (14 - 9) =$ _____

R. $(22 - 6) - 5 =$ _____   **N.** $(21 - 2) - (15 - 9) =$ _____

I. $(21 - 1) - (16 - 12) =$ _____   **O.** $(10 - 3) - (11 - 6) =$ _____

H. $(11 - 3) - 4 =$ _____

How many stars are in the Milky Way Galaxy?

‾‾‾‾ ‾‾‾ ‾‾‾   ‾‾‾ ‾‾‾ ‾‾‾ ‾‾‾ ‾‾‾ ‾‾‾ ‾‾‾   ‾‾‾ ‾‾‾ ‾‾‾ ‾‾‾ ‾‾‾ ‾‾‾ ‾‾‾
10   5   1   4   14   13   0   11   7   12   9   16   8   15   6   2   3

Name _____

Moon Madness

The answer to a subtraction problem is called the **difference**.

Subtract. Then write the ⌓ differences in order to answer the fun fact.

How fast does the moon travel in its orbit? _ _ _ _ m.p.h.

A. 11 – (15 – 9) = ____

14 – (18 – 9) = ____

B. (15 – 7) – (11 – 5) = ____

17 – (14 – 6) = ____

C. 16 – (15 – 8) = ____

18 – (16 – 7) = ____

D. 15 – (15 – 8) = ____

(16 – 8) – (10 – 4) = ____

E. (13 – 9) – (11 – 8) = ____

13 – (14 – 7) = ____

F. 12 – (13 – 6) = ____

17 – (12 – 3) = ____

G. (17 – 9) – (13 – 8) = ____

(15 – 6) – (12 – 5) = ____

H. 18 – (13 – 4) = ____

16 – (17 – 9) = ____

I. 14 – (13 – 5) = ____

15 – (16 – 8) = ____

J. 12 – (18 – 9) = ____

(20 – 7) – (6 – 2) = ____

On another piece of paper, write subtraction problems with a code to answer this question: What is the diameter of the moon? (2,160 miles) Have a friend solve the problems.

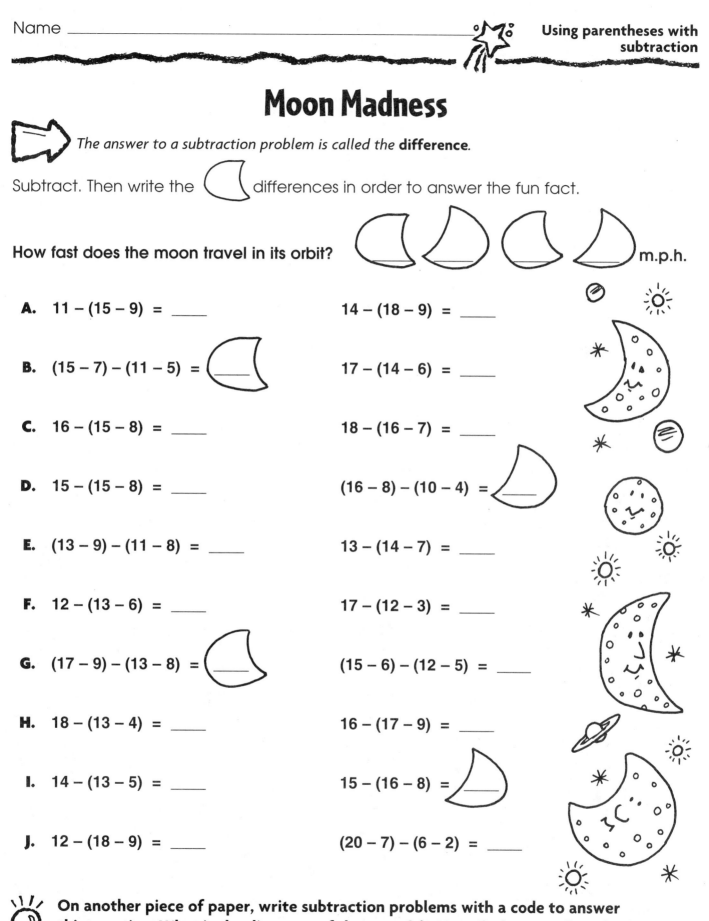

Chess, Anyone?

To subtract multiple-digit numbers without regrouping, follow these steps.

1. Subtract the ones column.	2. Subtract the tens column.	3. Subtract the hundreds column.	4. Subtract the thousands column.

```
   6,48⦗9⦘        6,4⦗8⦘9         6,⦗4⦘89         ⦗6⦘,489
 – 2,16⦗5⦘      – 2,1⦗6⦘5       – 2,⦗1⦘65       – ⦗2⦘,165
 ────────      ────────       ────────       ────────
        4            24            324         4,324
```

Subtract.

6,518 – 1,414	9,842 – 621	7,966 – 3,234	6,549 – 21
4,916 – 4,113	8,385 – 7,224	3,309 – 203	5,977 – 2,863
9,459 – 300	7,749 – 7,637	4,969 – 2,863	3,496 – 3,260
6,839 – 5,324	1,578 – 1,241	8,659 – 46	9,481 – 9,240

Checkmate

To subtract with regrouping, follow these steps.

1. Subtract the ones column. Regroup if needed.

```
  2 11
  4 ₿ ₹
-  2 6 6
        5
```

2. Subtract the tens column. Regroup if needed.

```
     12
  3 ₹ 11
   ₳ ₿ ₹
-  2 6 6
      6 5
```

3. Subtract the hundreds column. Regroup if needed.

```
     12
  3 ₹ 11
   ₳ ₿ ₹
-  2 6 6
    1 6 5
```

Subtract. Cross out the chess piece with the matching difference. The last piece standing is the winner of the match.

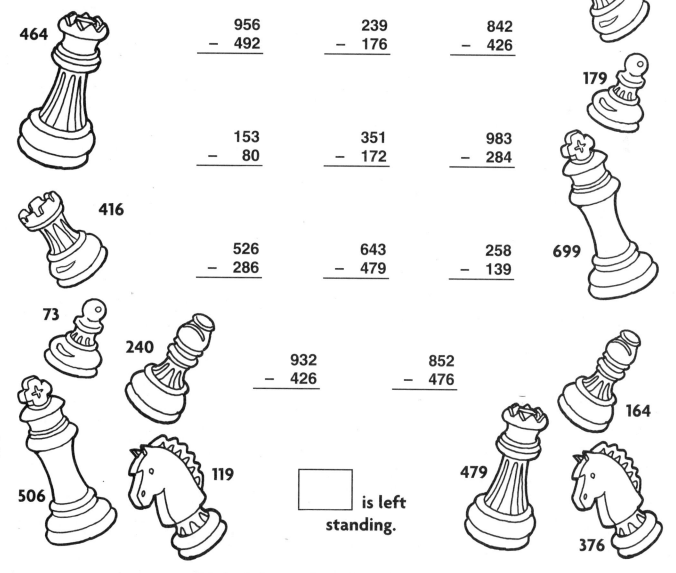

```
  956        239        842
- 492      - 176      - 426


  153        351        983
-  80      - 172      - 284


  526        643        258
- 286      - 479      - 139


  932        852
- 426      - 476
```

464   63   179   699   416   73   240   164   506   119   479   376

_____ is left standing.

Out of the Park!

To subtract with regrouping, follow these steps.

1.
$$
\begin{array}{r}
5\ 10 \\
3,4\cancel{6}\cancel{0} \\
-\quad 876 \\
\hline
4
\end{array}
$$

2.
$$
\begin{array}{r}
15 \\
3\cancel{5}\ 10 \\
3,\cancel{A}\cancel{6}\cancel{0} \\
-\quad 876 \\
\hline
84
\end{array}
$$

3.
$$
\begin{array}{r}
13\ 15 \\
2\ \cancel{3}\cancel{5}\ 10 \\
\cancel{3},\cancel{A}\cancel{6}\cancel{0} \\
-\quad 876 \\
\hline
584
\end{array}
$$

4.
$$
\begin{array}{r}
13\ 15 \\
2\ \cancel{3}\cancel{5}\ 10 \\
\cancel{3},\cancel{A}\cancel{6}\cancel{0} \\
-\quad 876 \\
\hline
2,584
\end{array}
$$

Subtract. Then use the code to solve the riddle below.

E.
$$
\begin{array}{r}
4,622 \\
-\ 1,284 \\
\hline
\end{array}
$$

E.
$$
\begin{array}{r}
5,198 \\
-\ \ 469 \\
\hline
\end{array}
$$

H.
$$
\begin{array}{r}
3,469 \\
-\ \ 890 \\
\hline
\end{array}
$$

T.
$$
\begin{array}{r}
6,077 \\
-\ 1,258 \\
\hline
\end{array}
$$

A.
$$
\begin{array}{r}
9,617 \\
-\ \ 759 \\
\hline
\end{array}
$$

R.
$$
\begin{array}{r}
3,804 \\
-\ \ 115 \\
\hline
\end{array}
$$

H.
$$
\begin{array}{r}
8,941 \\
-\ 1,895 \\
\hline
\end{array}
$$

N.
$$
\begin{array}{r}
952 \\
-\ \ 95 \\
\hline
\end{array}
$$

C.
$$
\begin{array}{r}
7,263 \\
-\ 4,772 \\
\hline
\end{array}
$$

B.
$$
\begin{array}{r}
7,603 \\
-\ 3,728 \\
\hline
\end{array}
$$

E.
$$
\begin{array}{r}
9,550 \\
-\ 4,298 \\
\hline
\end{array}
$$

L.
$$
\begin{array}{r}
6,451 \\
-\ \ 868 \\
\hline
\end{array}
$$

S.
$$
\begin{array}{r}
2,850 \\
-\ 1,976 \\
\hline
\end{array}
$$

I.
$$
\begin{array}{r}
2,972 \\
-\ \ 984 \\
\hline
\end{array}
$$

In what part of the ballpark do you find the whitest clothes?

___ ___   ___ ___ ___
1,988 857   4,819 2,579 5,252

___ ___ ___ ___ ___ ___ ___ ___ ___ !
3,875 5,583 4,729 8,858 2,491 7,046 3,338 3,689 874

💡 **On another piece of paper, write a subtraction problem that requires regrouping two times. Ask someone else to solve it.**

Touchdown!

Subtract. The final score of the game will be written in the footballs at the bottom of the page.

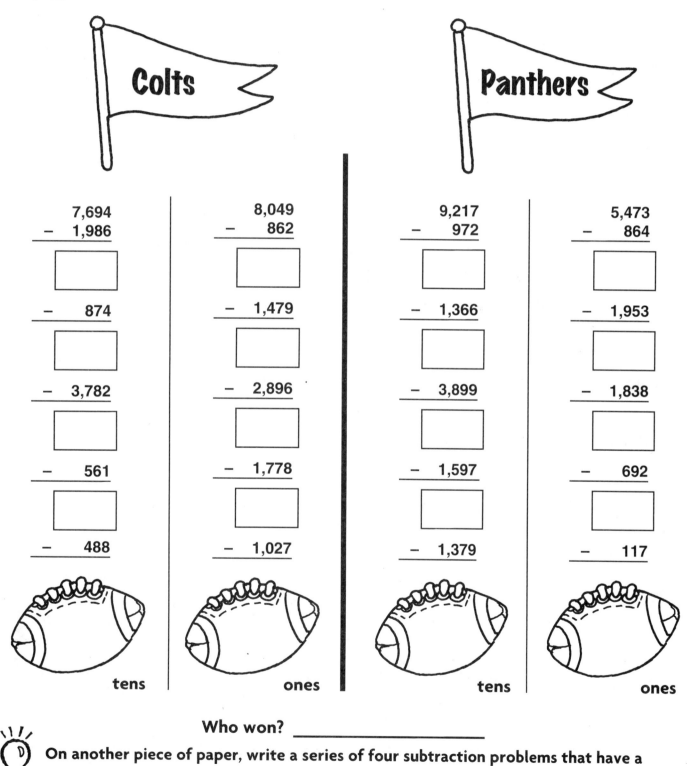

Colts

7,694 − 1,986	8,049 − 862
☐	☐
− 874	− 1,479
☐	☐
− 3,782	− 2,896
☐	☐
− 561	− 1,778
☐	☐
− 488	− 1,027

tens — **ones**

Panthers

9,217 − 972	5,473 − 864
☐	☐
− 1,366	− 1,953
☐	☐
− 3,899	− 1,838
☐	☐
− 1,597	− 692
☐	☐
− 1,379	− 117

tens — **ones**

Who won? _____

On another piece of paper, write a series of four subtraction problems that have a final difference equal to your age.

Name _____

A Funny Fixture

Continue regrouping into the ten thousands column if necessary.

Subtract. Then use the code to find the answer to the riddle below.

E. $\begin{array}{r} 63{,}210 \\ -\ 11{,}799 \end{array}$	I. $\begin{array}{r} 41{,}392 \\ -\ 38{,}164 \end{array}$	R. $\begin{array}{r} 76{,}146 \\ -\ 34{,}982 \end{array}$	E. $\begin{array}{r} 12{,}388 \\ -\ 9{,}891 \end{array}$
P. $\begin{array}{r} 54{,}391 \\ -\ 23{,}689 \end{array}$	H. $\begin{array}{r} 68{,}612 \\ -\ 59{,}446 \end{array}$	T. $\begin{array}{r} 97{,}413 \\ -\ 89{,}608 \end{array}$	L. $\begin{array}{r} 32{,}602 \\ -\ 19{,}561 \end{array}$
A. $\begin{array}{r} 18{,}546 \\ -\ 11{,}798 \end{array}$	G. $\begin{array}{r} 92{,}475 \\ -\ 76{,}097 \end{array}$	S. $\begin{array}{r} 29{,}816 \\ -\ 17{,}909 \end{array}$	! $\begin{array}{r} 78{,}752 \\ -\ 69{,}275 \end{array}$

Why did the man climb up the chandelier?

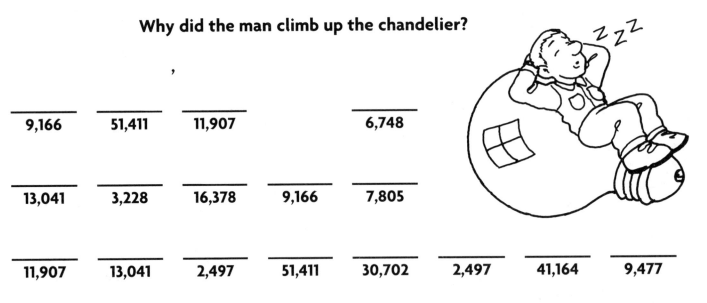

9,166	51,411	11,907		6,748	,

13,041	3,228	16,378	9,166	7,805

11,907	13,041	2,497	51,411	30,702	2,497	41,164	9,477

Bright Idea!

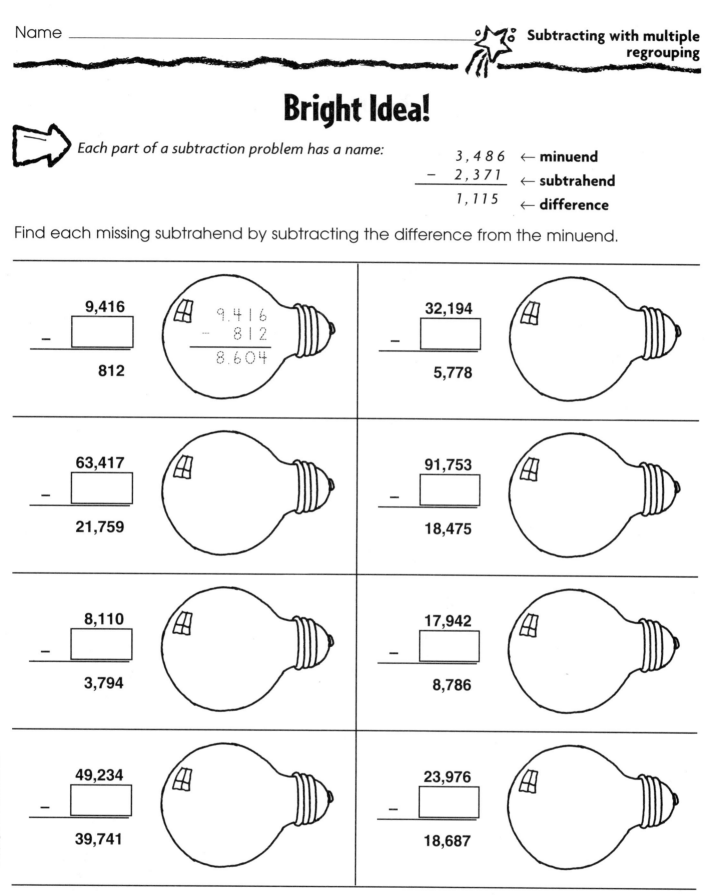

Each part of a subtraction problem has a name:

$$
\begin{array}{r}
3,486 \leftarrow \textbf{minuend} \\
- \quad 2,371 \leftarrow \textbf{subtrahend} \\
\hline
1,115 \leftarrow \textbf{difference}
\end{array}
$$

Find each missing subtrahend by subtracting the difference from the minuend.

9,416
−
812

9,416
− 812
8,604

32,194
−
5,778

63,417
−
21,759

91,753
−
18,475

8,110
−
3,794

17,942
−
8,786

49,234
−
39,741

23,976
−
18,687

On another piece of paper, write two subtraction problems with missing subtrahends. Ask a friend to solve the problems.

Map It Out

Always write a long subtraction problem vertically before solving it. When subtracting decimals, write each place value column so the decimal points are aligned.

$82.17 - 74.16 =$

$$\begin{array}{r} 82.71 \\ -\ 74.16 \\ \hline \end{array}$$

Write each subtraction problem vertically. Subtract.

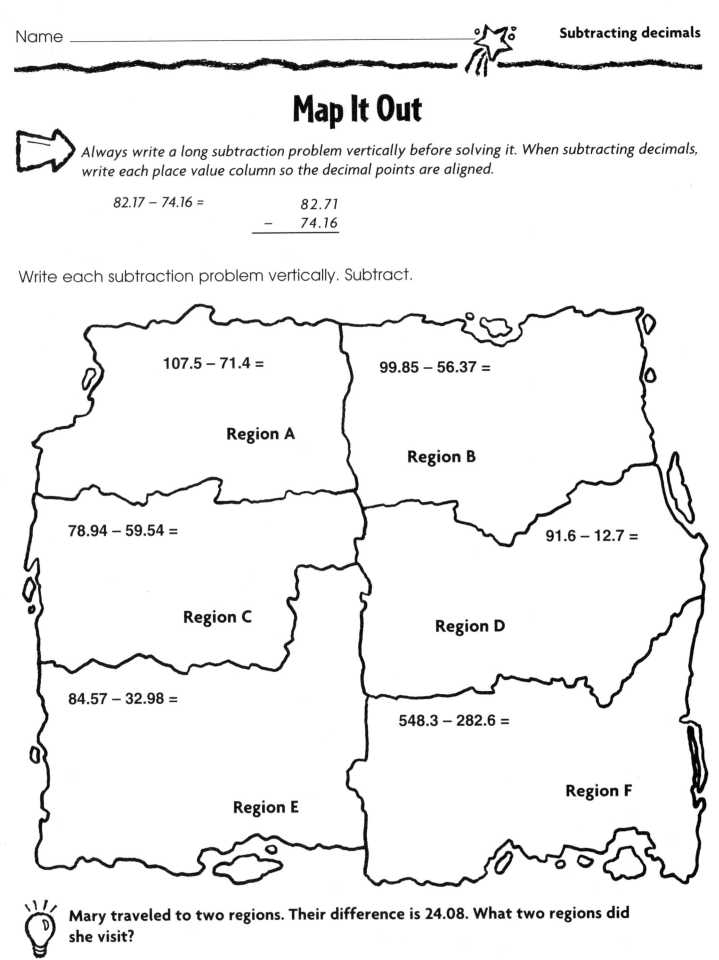

107.5 – 71.4 =

Region A

99.85 – 56.37 =

Region B

78.94 – 59.54 =

91.6 – 12.7 =

Region C

Region D

84.57 – 32.98 =

548.3 – 282.6 =

Region E

Region F

Mary traveled to two regions. Their difference is 24.08. What two regions did she visit?

Follow the Map

Write a number sentence for each problem. Solve.

A. Hannah's family drove 1,246 miles in 2 days. They drove 879 miles the first day. How far did they drive the second day?	**B.** Joplin is between Wells and Greenville. The distance from Wells to Greenville is 4,128 miles. The distance from Wells to Joplin is 1,839 miles. How far is it from Joplin to Greenville?
C. The Midnight Express travels 6,283 miles. When the train reaches Springfield, it has traveled 2,496 miles. How much farther will the Midnight Express travel?	**D.** Jacob's scout troop is going camping 947.6 miles from home. The bus breaks down after 289.9 miles. How far is the bus from the campgrounds?
E. Jonesburgh is between Johnsonville and Piper. Johnsonville is 8,612 miles from Piper. Piper is 4,985 miles from Jonesburgh. How far is it from Jonesburgh to Johnsonville?	**F.** Lola's family drove 2,391 miles to go to the beach. They drove home using another route that was 3,290 miles. How much longer was the second route?

It's a Circus in Here!

To multiply is to use repeated addition. Basic multiplication facts are learned by memorizing.

3 groups of 5 = 5 + 5 + 5 = 3 x 5 = 15

Multiply.

2 x 2	3 x 3	9 x 6	5 x 4	6 x 7
6 x 4	4 x 1	5 x 8	9 x 3	2 x 4
8 x 6	9 x 5	1 x 0	3 x 5	9 x 7
8 x 8	4 x 7	9 x 9	0 x 8	3 x 4
5 x 5	6 x 6	7 x 7	5 x 2	8 x 4

On another piece of paper, draw a picture to match this problem: There are 6 clowns. Each clown is holding 7 balloons. Then write the multiplication fact that tells the total number of balloons.

Under the Big Top

The answer to a multiplication problem is called the **product**.
The numbers being multiplied are called **factors**.

Multiply. Then use each product and the code to answer the riddles.

What happened to the human cannonball at the circus?

| 4 x 6 | 6 x 3 | | 7 x 7 | 3 x 4 | 8 x 8 | | 8 x 3 | 6 x 8 | 7 x 9 | 2 x 9 | 8 x 7 |

| 6 x 2 | 8 x 9 | 7 x 8 | | 9 x 9 | 8 x 6 | 9 x 7 | 3 x 6 | 7 x 8 | | 7 x 6 | 9 x 8 |

| 5 x 9 | 6 x 4 | 9 x 2 | | 8 x 8 | 4 x 3 | 6 x 6 | 6 x 3 | | 8 x 7 | 2 x 6 | 5 x 5 |!

What happened to the kid who ran away with the circus?

| 3 x 8 | 2 x 9 | | 4 x 6 | 3 x 4 | 8 x 7 |

| 9 x 5 | 6 x 7 | | 9 x 3 | 7 x 9 | 8 x 6 | 9 x 8 | 5 x 8 |

| 6 x 8 | 5 x 9 | | 3 x 9 | 2 x 6 | 5 x 3 | 9 x 6 |!

A = 12	H = 24	O = 42	
B = 27	I = 48	P = 16	V = 21
C = 15	J = 4	Q = 28	W = 49
D = 56	K = 54	R = 63	X = 1
E = 18	L = 8	S = 64	Y = 25
F = 81	M = 36	T = 45	Z = 2
G = 40	N = 72	U = 0	

Come to Costa Rica

To multiply with a 2-digit factor, follow these steps.

1. Multiply the ones column.

$$\begin{array}{r} 4|2 \\ \times |3 \\ \hline |6 \end{array}$$

2. Multiply the bottom factor in the ones column with the top factor in the tens column.

$$\begin{array}{r} 42 \\ \times 3 \\ \hline 126 \end{array}$$

Multiply. Use the code to fill in the blanks below.

I. 82 × 4	**O.** 91 × 9	**S.** 21 × 8	**H.** 92 × 3	**J.** 73 × 2
E. 71 × 7	**L.** 53 × 3	**R.** 90 × 8	**C.** 61 × 6	**N.** 11 × 5
A. 32 × 4	**F.** 41 × 9	**T.** 70 × 7	**E.** 52 × 4	**P.** 40 × 8

490 276 208

366 128 320 328 490 128 159

819 369 ___ 366 819 168 490 128

720 328 366 128 ___ 328 168

168 128 55 ___ 146 819 168 497 .

Costa Rica is in Central America. If a Costa Rican farmer sells 63 pounds of coffee every day for 3 days. How much will he sell altogether?

The Faraway Country

To multiply with a 2-digit factor that requires regrouping, follow these steps.

1. Multiply the ones.
    Regroup if needed.
    $7 \times 3 = 21$

2. Multiply the bottom factor in the ones column with
    the top factor in the tens column. Add the extra tens.
    $6 \times 3 = 18 \qquad 18 + 2 = 20$

Multiply.

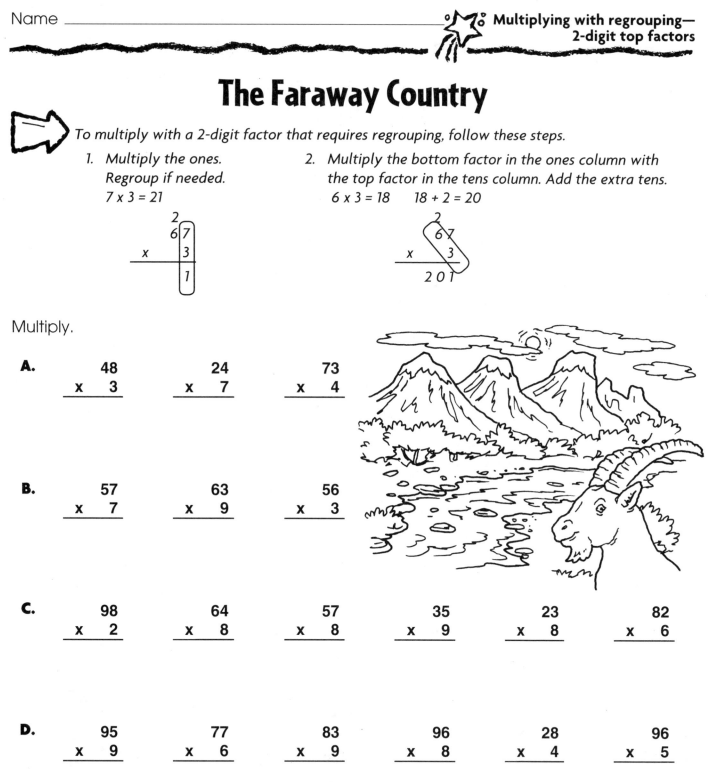

A.
$$\begin{array}{r} 48 \\ \times \quad 3 \\ \hline \end{array} \qquad \begin{array}{r} 24 \\ \times \quad 7 \\ \hline \end{array} \qquad \begin{array}{r} 73 \\ \times \quad 4 \\ \hline \end{array}$$

B.
$$\begin{array}{r} 57 \\ \times \quad 7 \\ \hline \end{array} \qquad \begin{array}{r} 63 \\ \times \quad 9 \\ \hline \end{array} \qquad \begin{array}{r} 56 \\ \times \quad 3 \\ \hline \end{array}$$

C.
$$\begin{array}{r} 98 \\ \times \quad 2 \\ \hline \end{array} \quad \begin{array}{r} 64 \\ \times \quad 8 \\ \hline \end{array} \quad \begin{array}{r} 57 \\ \times \quad 8 \\ \hline \end{array} \quad \begin{array}{r} 35 \\ \times \quad 9 \\ \hline \end{array} \quad \begin{array}{r} 23 \\ \times \quad 8 \\ \hline \end{array} \quad \begin{array}{r} 82 \\ \times \quad 6 \\ \hline \end{array}$$

D.
$$\begin{array}{r} 95 \\ \times \quad 9 \\ \hline \end{array} \quad \begin{array}{r} 77 \\ \times \quad 6 \\ \hline \end{array} \quad \begin{array}{r} 83 \\ \times \quad 9 \\ \hline \end{array} \quad \begin{array}{r} 96 \\ \times \quad 8 \\ \hline \end{array} \quad \begin{array}{r} 28 \\ \times \quad 4 \\ \hline \end{array} \quad \begin{array}{r} 96 \\ \times \quad 5 \\ \hline \end{array}$$

Switzerland is famous for the magnificent Swiss Alps. Waterfalls are formed by many of the mountain streams. To find out how many meters high one waterfall is, add the products in Row A.

A Changing Reef

To multiply with zeros, follow these steps.

| 90 x 2 | 9 x 2 = 18 Add a zero in the ones place to make 180. | 90 x 20 | 9 x 2 = 18 Add 2 zeros—one in the ones place and one in the tens place. | 900 x 20 | 9 x 2 = 18 Add 3 zeros—one in the ones place, one in the tens place, and one in the hundreds place. |

Multiply.

A.

| 80 x 7 | 60 x 50 | 900 x 30 | 40 x 11 | 120 x 2 | 200 x 60 |

B.

| 70 x 7 | 120 x 300 | 60 x 90 | 700 x 60 | 50 x 70 | 30 x 12 |

C.

| 600 x 80 | 40 x 12 | 30 x 8 | 90 x 50 | 200 x 120 | 50 x 8 |

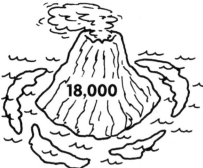

18,000

fringing reef

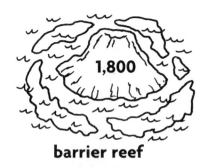

1,800

barrier reef

180

atoll

The formation of a coral reef starts growing around the top of an undersea volcano forming a fringing reef. As the volcano sinks, it leaves behind a barrier reef. When the volcano sinks below the ocean's surface, an atoll is left. On another piece of paper, write three problems with products to match those on the pictures.

Name _____

The Big City

To multiply with a 3-digit factor that requires regrouping, follow these steps.

1. Multiply the ones.
   Regroup if needed.

2. Multiply the tens in the top
   factor. Add the extra tens.
   Regroup if needed.

3. Multiply the hundreds in
   the top factor. Add the
   extra hundreds.

```
    1              4 1            4 1
  4 7 3          4 7 3          4 7 3
x     6        x     6        x     6
-------        -------        -------
    8            3 8          2,838
```

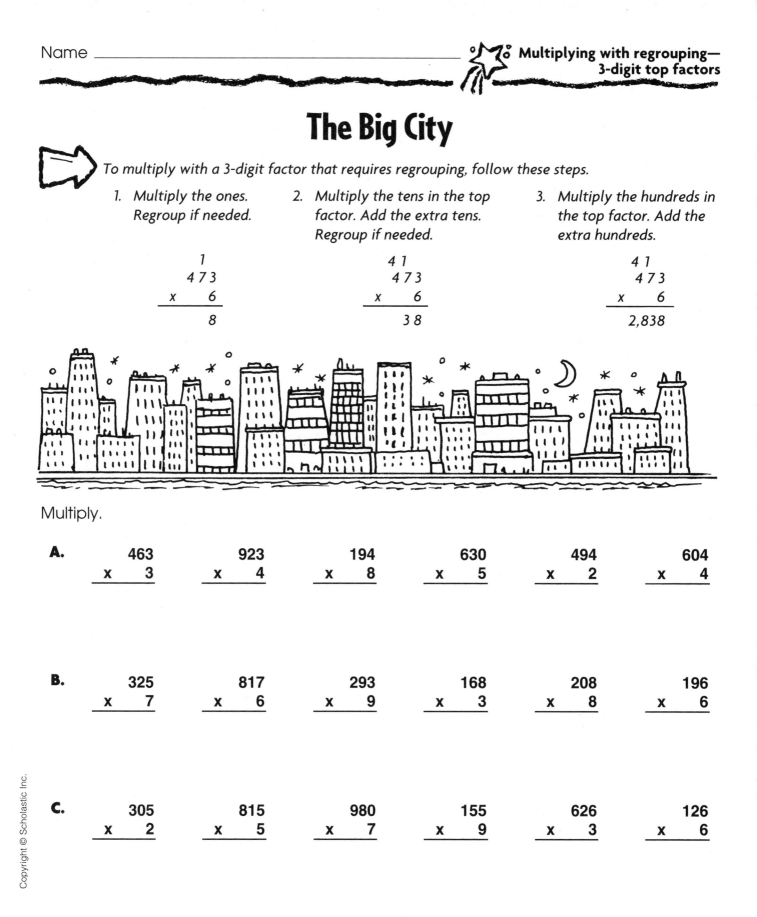

Multiply.

A.
```
    463          923          194          630          494          604
x     3        x     4      x     8      x     5      x     2      x     4
```

B.
```
    325          817          293          168          208          196
x     7        x     6      x     9      x     3      x     8      x     6
```

C.
```
    305          815          980          155          626          126
x     2        x     5      x     7      x     9      x     3      x     6
```

A subway train travels 296 miles daily. How far does the train travel in a week?

Stallions in the Stable

Multiply. Use the products to put each stallion back where he belongs. Write the horse's name on the stall door.

| 11,284 | 22,635 | 7,161 | 20,130 | 72,648 | 7,692 |

| 3,458
x 2 | 4,026
x 5 | 2,716
x 7 | 1,459
x 4 | 5,642
x 2 |

| | Lola's Lad | | | Stormy |

| 2,564
x 3 | 1,508
x 6 | 9,210
x 9 | 4,527
x 5 | 1,018
x 8 |

| Dusty | | | Black Beauty | |

| 1,809
x 7 | 2,387
x 3 | 9,081
x 8 | 7,186
x 4 | 7,130
x 6 |

| | Midnight | Lightning | | |

Stop Horsing Around!

To multiply with a 2-digit factor that requires regrouping, follow these steps.

1. Multiply by the ones digit.	2. Place a zero in the ones column..	3. Multiply by the tens digit.	4. Add to find the product.

```
      3                3                3              1
      46               46               46            3
    x 26             x 26             x 26           46
    ─────            ─────            ─────         x 26
     276              276              276         ─────
                        0            + 920          276
                                                  + 920
                                                  ─────
                                                  1,196
```

Multiply. Then use the code to answer the riddle below.

G. 32
    x 48

T. 67
    x 14

S. 53
    x 27

I. 96
    x 52

A. 83
    x 33

D. 49
    x 72

M. 39
    x 28

E. 56
    x 15

N. 83
    x 24

R. 75
    x 46

K. 96
    x 51

H. 84
    x 62

What horses like to stay up late?

___ ___ ___ ___ ___ ___ ___ ___ ___ ___!
1,992 4,992 1,536 5,208 938 1,092 2,739 3,450 840 1,431

💡 **Each of Farmer Gray's 24 horses eat 68 pounds of hay. How many pounds of hay do the horses eat altogether?**

Name _____

Famous Landmarks

Which of these landmarks is the tallest? Multiply. Write the ones digit of each product, in order, to find the height of each landmark. Circle the tallest landmark.

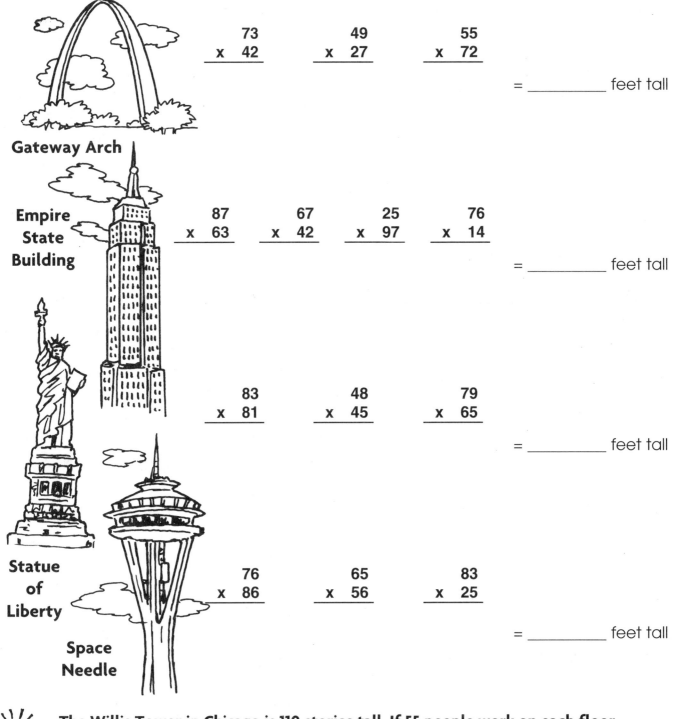

Gateway Arch

```
  73        49        55
x 42      x 27      x 72
```
= _____ feet tall

Empire State Building

```
  87        67        25        76
x 63      x 42      x 97      x 14
```
= _____ feet tall

```
  83        48        79
x 81      x 45      x 65
```
= _____ feet tall

Statue of Liberty

Space Needle

```
  76        65        83
x 86      x 56      x 25
```
= _____ feet tall

💡 **The Willis Tower in Chicago is 110 stories tall. If 55 people work on each floor, how many total people work in the building?**

Monumental Multiplication

Multiply.

A.

362	602	452	283	918	473
x 43	x 18	x 22	x 13	x 27	x 55

B.

540	417	308
x 38	x 56	x 61

C.

692	586	918
x 34	x 37	x 86

D.

467	598	861
x 42	x 29	x 73

The Washington Monument has 897 steps. If 42 people climb to the top, how many steps have they climbed altogether?

The Music Store

When a multiplication problem involves money, the product must have a dollar sign and a decimal point. The decimal point is placed between the ones digit and the tenths digit.

```
        6
        2
     $3.71
  x     94
  ───────
     14.84
  + 333.90
  ───────
   $348.84
```

Remember to use a dollar sign and a decimal point.

Multiply. Then use the code to answer the riddle below.

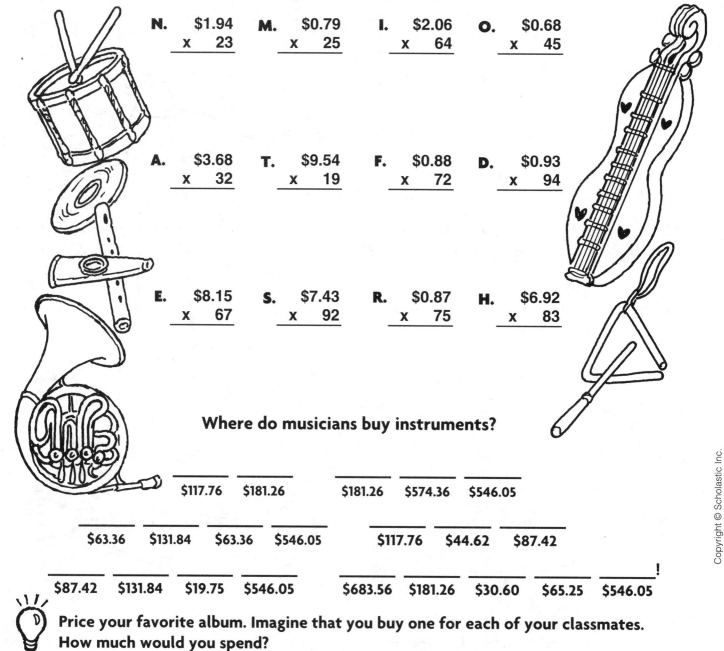

```
N.    $1.94      M.    $0.79      I.    $2.06      O.    $0.68
  x     23        x     25        x     64        x     45

A.    $3.68      T.    $9.54      F.    $0.88      D.    $0.93
  x     32        x     19        x     72        x     94

E.    $8.15      S.    $7.43      R.    $0.87      H.    $6.92
  x     67        x     92        x     75        x     83
```

Where do musicians buy instruments?

_____ _____   _____ _____ _____
$117.76 $181.26 $181.26 $574.36 $546.05

_____ _____ _____ _____   _____ _____ _____
$63.36 $131.84 $63.36 $546.05 $117.76 $44.62 $87.42

_____ _____ _____ _____   _____ _____ _____ _____ _____!
$87.42 $131.84 $19.75 $546.05 $683.56 $181.26 $30.60 $65.25 $546.05

Price your favorite album. Imagine that you buy one for each of your classmates. How much would you spend?

The Corner Candy Store

➡️ *Word problems that suggest equal groups often require multiplication.*

Write a number sentence for each problem. Solve.

A. Sam bought 4 candy bars at $1.23 each. How much did Sam spend altogether?	**B.** Mr. Johnson, the store owner, ordered 48 boxes of jawbreakers. Each box contained 392 pieces of candy. How many jawbreakers did Mr. Johnson order?
C. Carly's mom sent her to the candy store with 29 party bags. She asked Carly to fill each bag with 45 pieces of candy. How many pieces of candy will Carly buy?	**D.** Thirty-five children visited the candy store after school. Each child spent 57¢. How much money was spent in all?
E. Mr. Johnson keeps 37 jars behind the candy counter. Each jar contains 286 pieces of candy. How many pieces of candy are behind the counter altogether?	**F.** Nick bought each of his 6 friends a milk shake. Each milk shake cost $2.98. How much did Nick spend in all?

What's on the Tube?

➡ To divide means to make equal groups. Since multiplication also depends on equal groups, you can use the multiplication facts to help you learn the division facts.

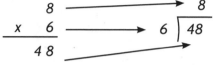

$$\begin{array}{r} 8 \\ \times\ 6 \\ \hline 4\,8 \end{array} \longrightarrow \quad 6\overline{)48}\ ^{8}$$

Basic division facts are problems you will learn by memory. Divide.

A. $4\overline{)24}$ $4\overline{)36}$ $7\overline{)56}$ $5\overline{)25}$ $9\overline{)81}$ $8\overline{)24}$

B. $5\overline{)45}$ $8\overline{)72}$ $4\overline{)28}$ $6\overline{)42}$ $6\overline{)36}$ $1\overline{)9}$

C. $3\overline{)12}$ $7\overline{)21}$ $6\overline{)48}$ $3\overline{)24}$ $8\overline{)32}$ $7\overline{)63}$

D. $8\overline{)64}$ $7\overline{)49}$ $5\overline{)30}$ $9\overline{)27}$ $6\overline{)6}$ $3\overline{)15}$

Divide to learn an interesting fact.

In what year was television invented?

$3\overline{)3}$ $8\overline{)72}$ $7\overline{)14}$ $8\overline{)56}$

💡 **Research to find the year something else was invented. On another piece of paper, write four division facts with the year hidden in their quotients.**

Television Division

Each part of a division problem has a name.

$$5 \leftarrow \text{quotient}$$
$$\text{divisor} \rightarrow 9\overline{)45} \leftarrow \text{dividend}$$

Divide.

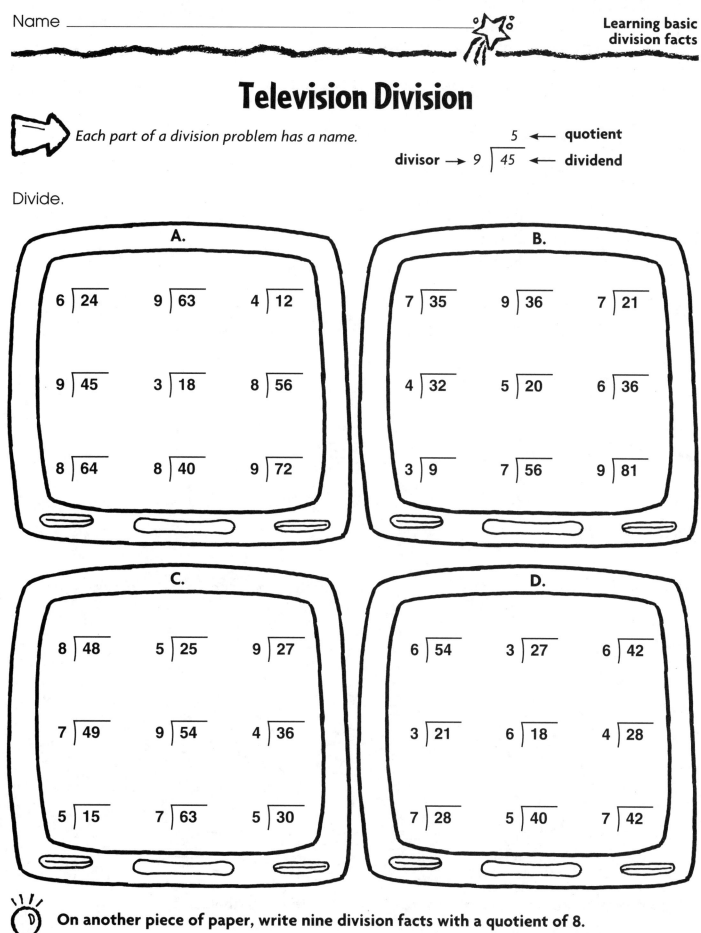

A.

$6\overline{)24}$ $9\overline{)63}$ $4\overline{)12}$

$9\overline{)45}$ $3\overline{)18}$ $8\overline{)56}$

$8\overline{)64}$ $8\overline{)40}$ $9\overline{)72}$

B.

$7\overline{)35}$ $9\overline{)36}$ $7\overline{)21}$

$4\overline{)32}$ $5\overline{)20}$ $6\overline{)36}$

$3\overline{)9}$ $7\overline{)56}$ $9\overline{)81}$

C.

$8\overline{)48}$ $5\overline{)25}$ $9\overline{)27}$

$7\overline{)49}$ $9\overline{)54}$ $4\overline{)36}$

$5\overline{)15}$ $7\overline{)63}$ $5\overline{)30}$

D.

$6\overline{)54}$ $3\overline{)27}$ $6\overline{)42}$

$3\overline{)21}$ $6\overline{)18}$ $4\overline{)28}$

$7\overline{)28}$ $5\overline{)40}$ $7\overline{)42}$

On another piece of paper, write nine division facts with a quotient of 8.

A Barrel of Monkeys

To divide with zeros, follow these samples.

$$\begin{array}{r} 80 \\ 8 \overline{)\,640} \end{array}$$ $64 \div 8 = 8$
$0 \div 8 = 0$
Add a zero to
make 80.

$$\begin{array}{r} 800 \\ 8 \overline{)\,6400} \end{array}$$ $64 \div 8 = 8$
$0 \div 8 = 0$
$0 \div 8 = 0$
Add 2 zeros to
make 800.

Divide.

A. $6 \overline{)\,420}$ $9 \overline{)\,8100}$ $6 \overline{)\,540}$ $5 \overline{)\,4500}$ $3 \overline{)\,2400}$

B. $3 \overline{)\,1800}$ $4 \overline{)\,320}$ $8 \overline{)\,7200}$ $7 \overline{)\,560}$ $5 \overline{)\,400}$

C. $3 \overline{)\,150}$ $4 \overline{)\,360}$ $6 \overline{)\,4800}$ $6 \overline{)\,360}$ $8 \overline{)\,640}$

90   **900**   **9**

Write three problems with quotients to match those on the barrels.

No Way!

To divide with remainders, follow these steps.

1. Does 8 x __ = 34? No!

$$8 \overline{)34}$$

2. Use the closest smaller dividend.
8 x 4 = 32

$$\begin{array}{r} 4 \\ 8 \overline{)34} \\ 32 \end{array}$$

3. Subtract to find the remainder.

$$\begin{array}{r} 4 \\ 8 \overline{)34} \\ -32 \\ \hline 2 \end{array}$$

4. The remainder is always less than the divisor.

$$\begin{array}{r} 4\ R2 \\ 8 \overline{)34} \\ -32 \\ \hline 2 \end{array}$$

Divide. Then use the code to complete the riddle below.

E. $9\overline{)84}$	L. $3\overline{)29}$	S. $7\overline{)67}$	O. $5\overline{)24}$
T. $6\overline{)23}$	N. $6\overline{)47}$	P. $6\overline{)39}$	I. $7\overline{)52}$
O. $4\overline{)19}$	A. $8\overline{)70}$	T. $3\overline{)26}$	S. $9\overline{)55}$
H. $4\overline{)23}$	! $7\overline{)45}$	R. $5\overline{)27}$	N. $8\overline{)79}$

Emily: **Yesterday I saw a man at the mall with very long arms. Every time he went up the stairs he stepped on them.**

Jack: **Wow! He stepped on his arms?**

Emily:

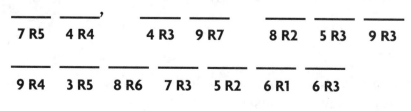

____ ____ ,   ____ ____   ____ ____ ____ ____
7 R5 4 R4   4 R3 9 R7   8 R2 5 R3 9 R3

____ ____ ____ ____ ____ ____ ____
9 R4 3 R5 8 R6 7 R3 5 R2 6 R1 6 R3

Name _____

Mousing Around

To divide with a 3-digit dividend, follow these steps.

1.
```
      6       7 x ___ = 42
  7 ) 427
      42      7 x 6 = 42
```

2.
```
      6       Subtract.
  7 ) 427
    - 42↓     Bring down
      07      the ones digit.
```

3.
```
      61      7 x ___ = 7
  7 ) 427
    - 42↓     7 x 1 = 7
      07      Subtract.
    -   7
       0
```

Divide. Then use the code to answer the riddle below.

T. 4) 208   U. 6) 306   H. 9) 819   C. 3) 246   A. 4) 368

E. 8) 648   O. 7) 497   S. 4) 248   N. 2) 168   D. 4) 288

C. 4) 328   I. 3) 159   W. 5) 305   M. 9) 279   ! 4) 88

Why did the cat hang out near the computer?

__ __   ___ __ __ __ __ __   __ __
53 52   61 92 84 52 81 72   52 71

__ __ __ __ __   __ __ __
82 92 52 82 91   52 91 81

__ __ __ __ __ __
31 71 51 62 81 22

On another piece of paper, design a mouse pad. Include at least three division problems and their quotients in your design.

Name _____

Surfing the Web

When the divisor has a remainder in the middle of a problem, follow these steps.

1.
$$8 \overline{)816}$$
$$\quad \frac{10}{80}$$
8 x ___ = 81
8 x 10 = 80

2.
$$8 \overline{)816}$$
$$\quad \frac{10}{-80\downarrow}$$
$$\quad \quad 16$$
Subtract.
Bring down the ones digit.

3.
$$8 \overline{)816}$$
$$\quad \frac{102}{-42\downarrow}$$
$$\quad \quad 07$$
$$\quad \quad \frac{-7}{0}$$
8 x ___ = 16
8 x 2 = 16
Subtract again.

Divide. Use another piece of paper to work the problems.
Then connect each problem to its answer to learn the definitions of some computer terms.

A. $5 \overline{)375}$ browser

B. $6 \overline{)492}$ byte

C. $2 \overline{)216}$ download

D. $3 \overline{)249}$ gigabyte

E. $9 \overline{)243}$ Internet

F. $8 \overline{)288}$ megabyte

G. $4 \overline{)424}$ network

H. $6 \overline{)564}$ program

I. $7 \overline{)532}$ scanner

J. $4 \overline{)312}$ virus

K. $9 \overline{)486}$ web site

82   an amount of data equal to 8 bits

75   a program to help get around the Internet

54   a place on the Internet's World Wide Web where text and pictures are stored

106   a group of computers linked together so they can share information

36   an amount of information equal to 1,048,516 bytes

27   a worldwide system of linked computers

108   to transfer information from a host computer to a personal computer

83   an amount of information equal to 1,024 megabytes

78   a program that damages other programs and data; often transmitted through telephone lines or shared disks

94   instructions for a computer to follow

76   a device that can transfer words and pictures from a printed page into the computer

Poolside!

Remember: The remainder is always less than the divisor.

Divide. Then use the code to answer the riddle below.

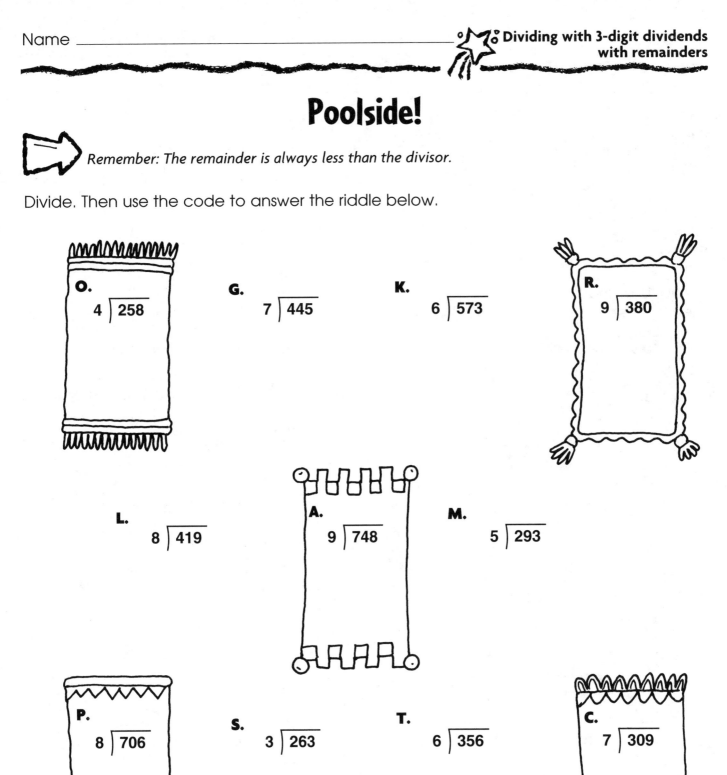

O. 4) 258

G. 7) 445

K. 6) 573

R. 9) 380

L. 8) 419

A. 9) 748

M. 5) 293

P. 8) 706

S. 3) 263

T. 6) 356

C. 7) 309

What kind of pool is not made for swimming?

____ ____ ____ ____ ____ ____ ____ ____ !
83R1 44R1 83R1 42R2 88R2 64R2 64R2 52R3

Summer Days

Divide. Then use the code to answer the riddle below.

Z. 3⟌2226   **N.** 5⟌2918   **T.** 8⟌2099

S. 4⟌2992   **B.** 7⟌4332   **P.** 9⟌3204

D. 6⟌2364   **C.** 7⟌3800   **U.** 3⟌2571

O. 9⟌8289   **A.** 5⟌4609   **Y.** 8⟌5376

What is the best day to go to the beach?

___ ___ ___ ___ ___ ___!
748   857   583R3   394   921R4   672

💡 **A year has 365 days. Summer is one of the four seasons. On another piece of paper, divide to find the exact number of days that are in each season. Your answer will tell you why our seasons truly change at a specific hour.**

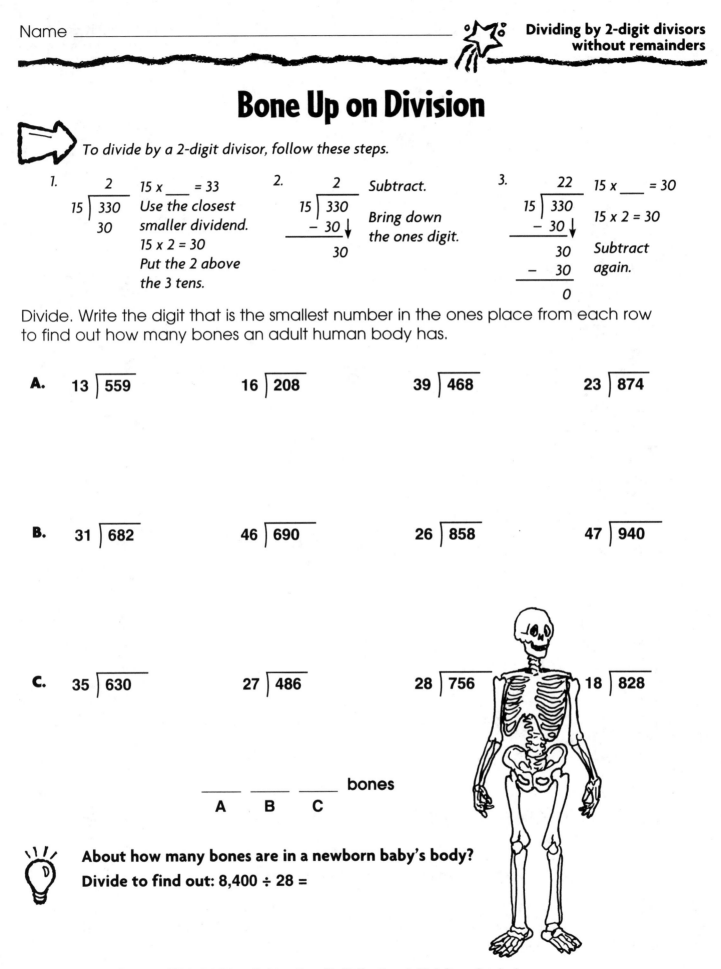

Bone Up on Division

To divide by a 2-digit divisor, follow these steps.

1.
$$\begin{array}{r} 2 \\ 15 \overline{\smash{\big)}\,330} \\ 30 \end{array}$$
15 x ___ = 33
Use the closest
smaller dividend.
15 x 2 = 30
Put the 2 above
the 3 tens.

2.
$$\begin{array}{r} 2 \\ 15 \overline{\smash{\big)}\,330} \\ -\ 30\downarrow \\ \hline 30 \end{array}$$
Subtract.

Bring down
the ones digit.

3.
$$\begin{array}{r} 22 \\ 15 \overline{\smash{\big)}\,330} \\ -\ 30\downarrow \\ \hline 30 \\ -\ 30 \\ \hline 0 \end{array}$$
15 x ___ = 30
15 x 2 = 30

Subtract
again.

Divide. Write the digit that is the smallest number in the ones place from each row
to find out how many bones an adult human body has.

A. 13) 559   16) 208   39) 468   23) 874

B. 31) 682   46) 690   26) 858   47) 940

C. 35) 630   27) 486   28) 756   18) 828

___ ___ ___ **bones**
A   B   C

About how many bones are in a newborn baby's body?
Divide to find out: 8,400 ÷ 28 =

Let's Go to the Show

Look at each sample to learn how to finish dividing when there is a zero in the quotient.

Sample 1:

```
        306
    8 ) 2448
      - 24↓
        04↓
       - 0↓
        48
       - 48
```

8 x ___ = 4
Since there is no
number, record a
0 in the quotient.
Subtract and
bring down the 8.
Continue to divide.

Sample 2:

```
        680
    6 ) 4080
      - 36↓
        048↓
       - 48
        00
```

Sample 3:

```
        20 R9
   44 ) 889
      - 88↓
        09
       - 0
         9
```

Divide. Then use the code to answer the riddle below.

S. 3) 1812   **U.** 4) 3632   **W.** 18) 910   **X.** 25) 3250

G. 17) 356   **B.** 6) 1848   **R.** 39) 786   **J.** 8) 7216

A. 7) 4207   **E.** 27) 562   **Y.** 9) 2880   **T.** 9) 6345

What is the name of the movie about frogs in outer space?

___ ___ ___ ___   ___ ___ ___ ___ ___ !
604 705 601 20R6 50R10 601 20R6 705 604

Imagine that you have popped 1,422 pieces of popcorn for you and your 5 friends.
How many pieces would each person get?

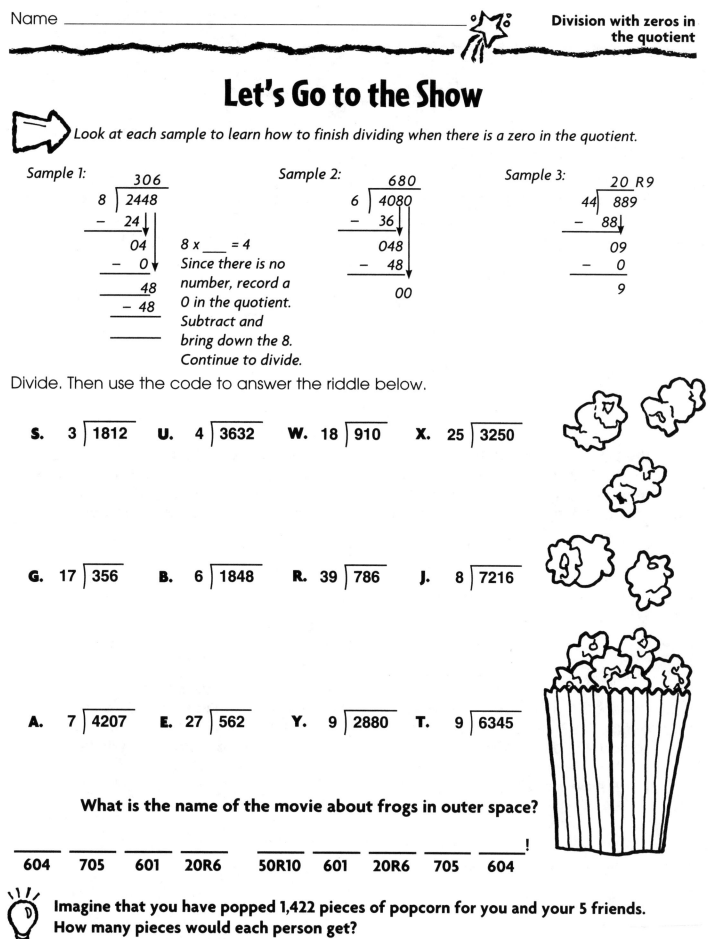

On the Big Screen

Word problems that give you a large group and ask you to make smaller, equal groups require division. Write a division problem. Solve.

A. The movie theater holds 988 people. It has 38 rows with an equal number of seats. How many seats are in each row?	**B.** A box of popcorn holds 972 kernels. If 18 friends share a box equally, how many kernels will each friend get?
C. The box office sold 4,020 tickets to 6 shows. The same number of people attended each show. How many tickets did they sell to each show?	**D.** The theater sold 4,315 tickets over 5 days. The same number of tickets were sold each day. How many tickets did they sell each day?
E. The soda fountain serves 7 types of drinks. On Saturday night, the theater served 952 drinks of the 7 drinks in equal amounts. How many drinks of each type were served?	**F.** The ticket office had 657 extra tickets. They were donated equally to 9 charities. How many tickets did each charity receive?

Page 4
A. 13, 14; B. 18, 14; C. 16, 12;
D. 15,14; E. 15, 15; F. 15, 13; G. 17,
17; H. 19, 15; I. 17, 14; J. 15, 20;
K. 20, 22; (6 + 3) + 7=16 pieces

Page 5

18	18	17	19	15
16	18	15	15	17
17	18	18	16	16
17	22	18	15	19
17	15	18	18	18

Page 6
A. 3,569, 9,876; B. 9,982, 7,949,
7,860, 91,798; C. 86,992, 90,749,
89,994, 77,787; D. 581,998,
774,862, 567,990, 694,939,
959,596; 29,029 feet

Page 7
A. 15,981, **19,341**, 10,397, 8,990;
B. **12,218**, 12,188, 11,929,10,984;
C. 18,990, 16,767, **20,322**, 16,971;
D. 17,759, 15,984, 14,487, **18,510**;
39,661 feet

Page 8
Z. 1,371; B. 632; R. 1,211; Q.
1,522; S. 1,201; X. 761; I. 9,107;
C. 4,053; Y. 10,155; A. 14,024;
Y. 9,122; L. 103,468; P. 76,076;
E. 82,373; F. 92,228; D. 539,396;
Q. 651,951; R. 1,059,472; THEY
ARE BIRDS OF PREY.

Page 9
H. 9,122; L. 12,548; I. 18,975;
A. 17,531; E. 10,322; O. 17,200;
C. 18,506; T. 14,123; M. 13,590;
N. 130,752; U. 111,110; Y. 182,920;
R. 136,131; THE BALD EAGLE IS
FOUND ONLY ON THE NORTH
AMERICAN CONTINENT.

Page 10
W. 7,901; T. 12,300; P. 7,148;
N. 12,885; O. 11,695; E. 15,019;
H. 15,994; R. 10,404; S. 9,207;
! 9,816; A. 8,915; U. 11,303; ONE
WEARS TROUSERS. THE OTHER
PANTS!

Page 11
A. 6,741 + **3**,382 = 10,123, 9,443
+ 9,**8**17 = 19,260, **4**,578 + 5,361 =
9,939, **2**,227 + 6,**9**73 = 9,200;
B. 3,841 + **4**,064 = 7,905, 7,024 +
9,**4**38 = 16,462, **9**,**8**10 + 9,385 =
19,195, **7**,426 + 7,92**3** = 15,349;
C. 1,**7**73 + 1**5**8 = 1,931, 3,**6**54 +
6,474 = 10,128, **4**,284 + 3,**8**21 =
8,105, 8,**8**63 + **2**,317 = 11,180;
D. 3,**9**48 + 9,**2**65 = 13,213, **9**,**7**59
+ 8,**7**24 = 18,483, 7,558 + **9**,**9**48
= 17,506, 4,**5**95 + **6**,628 = 11,223;
38,**3**69 + 4**2**,510 = 80,879 pieces

Page 12
A. $92.83; G. $92.53; U $114.60;
O. $63.87; B. $72.25; N. $170.78;
E. $157.35; R. $69.37; M. $168.72;
C. $765.09; S. $980.05; T. $670.09;
D. $477.07; Y. $616.34;
F. $1,216.40; W. $1,000.68;
BECAUSE MONEY DOESN'T
GROW ON TREES!

Page 13
A. $69.95; B. $118.00; C. $23.88;
D. $18.58; E. $178.75; F. $5.25

Page 14
N. 3; T. 10; B. 9; L. 15; U. 14; E. 7;
D. 0; O. 1; L. 8; I. 6; W. 5; D. 12;
R. 11; N. 13; I. 16; O. 2; H. 4; TWO
HUNDRED BILLION

Page 15
2237 m.p.h.; A. 5, 5; B. 2, 9; C. 9,
9; D. 8, 2; E. 1, 6; F. 5, 8; G. 3, 2;
H. 9, 8; I. 6, 7; J. 3, 9

Page 16
5,104, 9,221, 4,732, 6,528; 803,
1,161, 3,106, 3,114; 9,159, 112,
2,106, 236; 1,515, 337, 8,613, 241

Page 17
464, 63, 416; 73, 179, 699; 240,
164, 119; 506, 376;
479 is left standing.

Page 18
E. 3,338; E. 4,729; H. 2,579;
T. 4,819; A. 8,858; R. 3,689;
H. 7,046; N. 857; C. 2,491; B.
3,875; E. 5,252; L. 5,583; S. 874;
I. 1,988; IN THE BLEACHERS!

Page 19
First Column: 5,708, 4,834, 1,052,
491, 3; Second Column: 7,187,
5,708, 2,812, 1,034, 7; Third
Column: 8,245, 6,879, 2,980, 1,383,
4; Fourth Column: 4,609, 2,656,
818, 126, 9; Panthers

Page 20
E. 51,411; I. 3,228; R. 41,164;
E. 2,497; P. 30,702; H. 9,166;
T. 7,805; L. 13,041; A. 6,748;
G. 16,378; S. 11,907; ! 9,477;
HE'S A LIGHT SLEEPER!

Page 21
8,604; 26,416; 41,658; 73,278;
4,316; 9,156; 9,493; 5,289

Page 22
A. 36.1; B. 43.48; C. 19.40; D. 78.9;
E. 51.59; 265.7; Mary visited
Regions B and C.

Page 23
A. 1,246 − 879 = 367 miles;
B. 4,128 − 1,839 = 2,289 miles;
C. 6,283 − 2,496 = 3,787 miles;
D. 947.6 − 289.9 = 657.7 miles;
E. 8,612 − 4,985 = 3,627 miles;
F. 3,290 − 2,391 = 899 miles

Page 24
4, 9, 54, 20, 42; 24, 4, 40, 27, 8; 48,
45, 0, 15, 63; 64, 28, 81, 0, 12; 25,
36, 49, 10, 32; 6 x 7 = 42 balloons

Page 25
HE WAS HIRED AND FIRED ON
THE SAME DAY!; HE HAD TO
BRING IT BACK!

Page 26
I. 328; O. 819; S. 168; H. 276;
J. 146; E. 497; L. 159; R. 720;
C. 366; N. 55; A. 128; F. 369;
T. 490; E. 208; P. 320; THE
CAPITAL OF COSTA RICA IS SAN
JOSE.; 189 pounds of coffee

Page 27
A. 144, 168, 292; B. 399, 567, 168;
C. 196, 512, 456, 315, 184, 492;
D. 855, 462, 747, 768, 112, 480;
604 meters

Page 28

A.560, 3,000, 27,000, 440, 240, 12,000; B. 290, 36,000, 5,400, 42,000, 3,500, 360; C. 48;000, 480, 240, 4,500, 24,000, 400

Page 29

A. 1,389, 3,692, 1,552, 3,150, 988, 2,416; B. 2,275, 4,902, 2,637, 504, 1,664, 1,176; C. 610, 4,075, 6,860, 1,395, 1,878, 756; 2,072 miles

Page 30

6,916, 20,130, 19,012, 5,836, 11,284; 7,692, 9,048, 82,890, 22,635, 8,144; 12,663, 7,161, 72,648, 28,744, 42,780; Stormy, Black Beauty, Midnight, Lola's Lad, Lightning, Dusty

Page 31

G. 1,536; T. 938; S. 1,431; I. 4,992; A. 2,739; D. 3,528; M. 1,092; E. 840; N. 1,992; R. 3,450; K. 4,896; H. 5,208; NIGHTMARES!; 1,632 pounds

Page 32

3,066, 1,323, 3,960; 630 feet; 5,481, 2,814, 2,425, 1,064; 1,454 feet; 6,723, 2,160, 5,135; 305 feet; 6,536, 3,640, 2,075; 605 feet; Empire State Building should be circled.; 6,050 people

Page 33

A. 15,566, 10,836, 9,944, 3,679, 24,786, 26,015; B. 20,520, 23,352, 18,788; C. 23,528, 21,682, 78,948; D. 19,614, 17,342, 62,853; 37,674 steps

Page 34

A. $44.62; M. $19.75; I. $131.84; O. $30.60; A. $117.76; T. $181.26; F. $63.36; D. $87.42; E. $546.05; S. $683.56; R. $65.25; H. $574.36; AT THE FIFE AND DIME STORE!

Page 35

A. $4.92; B. 18,816; C. 1,305; D. $19.95; E. 10,582; F. $17.88

Page 36

A. 6, 9, 8, 5, 9, 3; B. 9, 9, 7, 7, 6, 9; C. 4, 3, 8, 8, 4, 9, D. 8, 7, 6, 3, 1, 5; 1927

Page 37

A. 4, 7, 3, 5, 6, 7, 8, 5, 8; B. 5, 4, 3, 8, 4, 6, 3, 8, 9; C. 6, 5, 3, 7, 6, 9, 3, 9, 6; D. 9, 9, 7, 7, 3, 7, 4, 8, 6

Page 38

A. 70, 900, 90, 900, 800; B. 600, 80, 900, 80, 80; C. 50, 90, 800, 60, 80

Page 39

E. 9 R3; L. 9 R2; S. 9 R4; O. 4 R4; T. 3 R5; N. 7 R5; P. 6 R3; I. 7 R3; O. 4 R3; A. 8 R6; T. 8 R2; S. 6 R1; H. 5 R3; ! 6 R3; R. 5 R2; N. 9 R7; NO, ON THE STAIRS!

Page 40

T. 52; U. 51; M. 91; C. 82; A. 92; E. 81; O. 71; S. 62; N. 84; D. 72; C. 82; I. 53; W. 61; M. 31; ! 22; IT WANTED TO CATCH THE MOUSE!

Page 41

A. 75; B. 82; C. 108; D. 83; E. 27; F. 36; G. 106; H. 94; I. 76; J. 78; K. 54

Page 42

O. 64 R2; G. 63 R4; K. 95 R3; R. 42 R2; L. 52 R3; A. 83 R1; M. 58 R3; P. 88 R2; S. 87 R2; T. 59 R2; C. 44 R1; A CARPOOL!

Page 43

Z. 742; N. 583 R3; T. 262 R3; S. 748; B. 618 R6; P. 356; D. 394; C. 542 R6; U. 857; O. 921; A. 921 R4; Y. 672; SUNDAY!; 91 R1 days

Page 44

A. 43, 13, 12, 38; B. 22, 15, 33, 20; C. 18, 18, 27, 46; 206 bones; 300 bones

Page 45

S. 604; U. 908; W. 50 R10; X. 130; G. 20 R16; B. 308; R. 20 R6; J. 902; A. 601; E. 20 R22; Y. 320; T. 705; STAR WARTS!; 237 pieces of popcorn

Page 46

A. 26 seats; B. 54 kernels; C. 670 tickets; D. 863 tickets; E. 136 drinks; 73 tickets